Badminton
Handbook

by Sandra Stevenson

HANCOCK HOUSE PUBLISHERS

ISBN 0-88839-041-6 pa.

Copyright © 1980 Stevenson, Sandra

These books have been prepared for the Ministry of Education, Province of British Columbia, under the direction of the Secondary Physical Education Curriculum Revision Committee (1980)

James Appleby	John Lowther
Alex Carre	Mike McKee
Madeline Gemmill	Norman Olenick
Gerry Gilmore	David Turkington
George Longstaff	

Handbook consultant: F. Alex Carre, Ph.D.

Acknowledgments

Many thanks to all those who helped to enrich my badminton career. You have made this manual possible.

Cataloguing in Publication Data

Stevenson, Sandra.
    Badminton handbook and curriculum guide
(Physical education series)

    Bibliography: p.

    1. Badminton (Game) - Training. I. Title.
II. Series: Physical Education Series (North Vancouver, B.C.)
GV1007.S74   796.34'5'0712   C80-091142-3

All rights reserved. No part of this publication may be reproduced, stored in a retrieval system or transmitted in any form or by any means, electronic, mechanical, photocopying, recording or otherwise without the prior written permission of Hancock House Publishers.

Editor Margaret Campbell
Design Paul Willies & Donna White
Production Tom Morgan
Cover Photo Paul Bond
Typeset by Donna White *in Megaron type on an AM Varityper Comp/Edit*

Second Printing 1982

Published by
HANCOCK HOUSE PUBLISHERS
1431 Harrison Avenue, Blaine, WA, U.S.A. 98230
256 Route 81, Killingworth, CT, U.S.A. 06417
HANCOCK HOUSE PUBLISHERS LTD.
19313 Zero Avenue, Surrey, B.C., Canada V3S 5J9

Table of Contents

Acknowledgements 2

Chapter One
Format and Purpose of the Handbook
   A. Introduction 5
   B. Purpose of the Handbook 5
   C. Handbook Format 5
   D. Objectives of the Program 5
   E. Application to Classroom Teaching 5
   F. Description of the Levels Approach 6
   G. Explanation of Activity Sequence Chart 6
   H. Activity Sequence Chart 6
   I. Relationship of Badminton to Goals and Learning Outcomes 8
      Court Diagram 8

   Chapter Two
Skill Development: Teaching Techniques and Definitions
   A. Basic Skills 9
      1. Underarm Forehand 9
      2. Underarm Backhand 10
      3. Service 11
         a) Governing Rules 11
         b) Short Serve 11
         c) High Serve 12
      4. Forehand Overhead Clear 13
      5. Net Shots 14
         a) Upward Net Shot 14
         b) Downward Net Shot 14
      6. Basic Footwork 14
         a) Ready Position 14
         b) Hitting Position 15
   B. Refined Strokes 16
      1. Overhead Drop Shot 16
      2. Smash 16
      3. Smash Return 17
      4. Backhand Overhead Clear 18
      5. Stroke Variation 18
   C. Rules 20
      1. Start of Game 20
      2. Game 21
      3. Faults 21
      4. General Rules 22

    D. Tactics 22
        1. Mental Discipline 22
        2. Game Tactics 23
            a) Defensive and Offensive Play 23
            b) Serve and Serve Return 23
            c) Specific Tactics in Singles 24
            d) Specific Tactics in Doubles 25
            e) Specific Tactics in Mixed Doubles 26

Chapter Three

Drills

    A. Practice Drills for Basic Underarm Strokes 28
    B. Service Drills 29
    C. Forehand Overhead Clear Drills 29
    D. Running Drills (Footwork Practice) 30
    E. Net Shot Drills 31
    F. Overhead Drop Shot Drills 31
    G. Smash and Smash Return Drills 31
    H. Backhand Overhead Clear Drills 31
    I. Modified Games 32

Chapter Four

Sample Lesson Plans

    Lesson One: Introduction. 33
    Lesson Two: Basic Underarm Strokes. 34
    Lesson Three: Underhand and Overhead Basic Strokes. 34
    Lesson Four: Game Rules. 34
    Lesson Five: Skills Test Practice. 35
    Lesson Six: Evaluation of Court Skills. 35
    Lesson Seven: Overhead Drop and Smash. 35
    Lesson Eight: Strategy (Multi-Level Lesson) 36
    Lesson Nine: Review (Multi-Level Lesson) 36

Chapter Five

Evaluation

    A. Program Evaluation 37
    B. Player Evaluation 37
        1. Psychomotor Evaluation 37
        2. Cognitive Evaluation 38
        3. Affective Evaluation 38

Appendix I   Reference Material 39
Appendix II   National Test Program 40

Chapter One
Format And Purpose Of The Handbook

A. Introduction

One of the primary aims of the Badminton program should be to encourage players to continue the sport after the school program either in a community recreation program or through a badminton club. Badminton is an excellent lifelong recreational activity which can improve physical fitness and is also an enjoyable activity.

B. Purpose of the Handbook

This handbook is an extension of the Physical Education Curriculum and Resource Guide (1980). The material included in the handbook is designed to provide the instructor with a comprehensive source of information for the teaching of Badminton.

C. Handbook Format

This handbook uses a developmental focus that emphasizes individual instruction within a large group situation, while at the same time outlining a Levels approach which allows the instructor to work with players of varying skills. Skill development sequence is outlined in the Activity Sequence Chart, and corresponds closely with coaches' manuals distributed by the Canadian Badminton Association. Many players continue to play badminton at private clubs or community centers affiliated with the CBA, and using their coaching manuals as a guideline will help standardize school instruction with that offered elsewhere.

The handbook describes in detail the skills required for playing Badminton and the recommended techniques for teaching them. It suggests drills which can be used to practice these skills, offers sample lesson plans for the use of the instructors and discusses methods of evaluation. The guidelines presented in this handbook are suggestions only and may be adapted as the instructor becomes more familiar with Badminton.

D. Objectives of the Program

The objectives of this program are to introduce players to the fundamental skills and rules of Badminton while at the same time offering them an option for a lifetime personal sport. These skills include:

1. Psychomotor skills
2. Cognitive skills
3. Affective skills

1. Psychomotor Objectives

Badminton is an excellent choice of activity for overall fitness since players engage in all the basic motor skills -- running, turning, jumping, hitting, throwing, as well as combinations of these activities. The sport also improves hand-eye coordination, flexibility and agility. The Chinese sum up the merits of good badminton players as "fast, fierce, fit and flexible."

2. Cognitive Objectives

   a) To teach players to think quickly and rationally in order to hit the shuttle correctly and to make split-second tactical decisions.
   b) To teach players to analyze and correct their movements through practice drills and modified games.
   c) To teach proper rules and etiquette of the game since Badminton is one of the few sports where players are expected to be their own linesmen and umpires.

3. Affective Objectives

   a) To teach self-discipline so that players learn to use their strengths to develop an effective game plan since no sideline coaching is allowed.
   b) To teach the value of an individual sport. Players learn to appreciate the discipline it takes to play an individual sport properly since there is no one on the court to compensate for them. Lack of proper skills, fitness or mental discipline will directly affect enjoyment and success in Badminton.
   c) To help players develop a positive attitude for becoming enthusiastically involved in the program.

E. Application To Classroom Teaching

1. Environment

The most suitable place to teach Badminton is a proper badminton hall or court complex where visibility and floor surface are not problems. The facility would have dark-colored walls and ceiling, and lights would be positioned between the courts. The floor would be clean and unwaxed. There should be a minimum of one meter (3 feet) behind the courts and 30 cm. (2 feet) between the courts.

In a class situation, it helps to have one court for every four players. A blackboard is a good teaching aid during group instruction.

2. Strategy

The primary reason for developing a teaching strategy is to encourage a positive attitude toward learning and toward the game of Badminton. In a Physical Education class, with players who have varying skill levels, the ability to organize a large group for individual activity can make the lesson a success or failure. The drills explained throughout this handbook are meant to be used with several players of different levels on a court. Since players tire quickly of straight skill practice, many modified games are included to teach skills in a game situation using only a portion of the court. An objective of good teaching strategy should be to make the lesson fun in order that the player has an enjoyable learning experience. In Chapter Two, application to classroom instruction will be dealt with as an extension of teaching techniques. Sample lesson plans are provided in Chapter Four.

F. Description of Levels Approach

In a comprehensive Physical Education curriculum, emphasis should be placed on the provision of a sound framework for individual development. One way of doing this is to use a sequentially developed program of physical activities that integrates affective, cognitive and psychomotor areas. This focus is called a "levels" approach.

The teaching of Badminton should begin with simple activities and progress to the more complex. However, progression is dependent on the individual player rather than being determined by any grade level. The levels approach has been developed to reinforce this concept.

Badminton uses a four-level system as follows:

Level I	- Beginner
Level II	- Novice
Level III	- Intermediate
Level IV	- Tournament (Advanced)

G. Explanation Of The Activity Sequence Chart

The activity sequence chart outlines a progressive pattern of skills required for Badminton. The chart serves as a reference, or sequence guide, in planning sessions and indicates the level at which each new skill should be introduced.

H. Activity Sequence Chart

SKILLS	LEVELS			
	I	II	III	IV
A. Basic Skills				
1. Underarm Forehand	●			
a) Grip	●			
b) Stroke Components	●			
i waiting position				
ii preparation				
iii point of contact				
iv follow-through				
c) Common Faults, Results and Correction	●			
2. Underarm Backhand	●			
a) Grip	●			
b) Stroke Components	●			
i waiting position				
ii preparation				
iii point of contact				
iv follow-through				
c) Common Faults, Results and Correction				
3. Service	●			
a) Governing Rules	●			
b) Short Serve	●			
i description				
ii stroke components				
iii Common Faults, Results and Correction				
c) High Serve	●			
i description				
ii stroke components				
iii Common Faults, Results and Correction				
4. Forehand Overhead Clear	●			
a) Description				
b) Stroke Components				
i stance				
ii weight transfer				
iii throwing action				
iv contact point				
v follow-through				
c) Common Faults, Results and Correction				
5. Net Shots	●			
a) Upward Net Shot	●			
i description				
ii stroke components				
iii Common Faults, Results and Correction				
b) Downward Net Shot	●			
i description				

SKILLS	LEVELS			
	I	II	III	IV
ii stroke components				
iii Common Faults, Results and Correction				
6. Basic Footwork	●			
a) Ready Position	●			
i description				
ii position components				
b) Hitting Position	●			
i description				
ii position components				
a) court movement				
b) body position				
c) overhead -balance, weight transfer				
d) net shots -balance, weight transfer				
iii Common Faults, Results and Correction				
B. Refined Strokes				
1. Overhead Drop Shot		●		
a) Description				
b) Stroke Components				
c) Common Faults, Results and Correction				
2. Smash		●		
a) Description				
b) Stroke Components				
i hitting action				
ii use of the body				
iii speed of the stroke				
c) Common Faults, Results and Correction				
3. Smash Return		●		
a) Description				
b) Stroke Components				
i waiting position				
ii footwork				
iii body position				
iv point of contact				
c) Common Faults, Results and Correction				
4. Backhand Overhand Clear		●		
a) Description				
b) Stroke Components				
i body position				

SKILLS	LEVELS			
	I	II	III	IV
ii arm action				
iii point of contact				
iv follow-through				
c) Common Faults, Results and Correction				
5. Stroke Variation				
a) Description				
b) Stroke Components				
i Flick Serve		●		
ii Drive Serve		●		
iii Underhand Drive		●		
iv Underhand Clear		●		
v Overhead Drive		●		
vi Backhand Drop		●		
vii Backhand Smash		●		
viii Overhead Cut Shots				●
ix Underhand Cut Shots				●
x Around the Head Clear			●	
C. Rules				
1. Basic Rules	●			
a) Start of the Game				
b) Game				
c) Faults				
d) General Rules				
D. Tactics				
1. Mental Discipline	●			
2. Game Tactics	●			
a) Defensive and Offensive Play	●			
i defensive shot				
ii offensive shot				
b) Serve and Serve Return		●		
i serve				
ii return of serve				
c) Specific Tactics in Singles		●		
i game play				
ii Common Mistakes, Results and Correction				
d) Specific Tactics in Doubles			●	
i game play				
ii Common Mistakes, Results and Correction				
e) Specific Tactics in Mixed Doubles				●
i game play				
ii Common Mistakes, Results and Correction				

I. Relationship of Badminton to Goals and Learning Outcomes

As a result of active participation in a Badminton program, players should realize the following goals:

1. An increase in their level of fitness and level of skill proficiency.
2. An increase in their level of understanding of the game and its psychomotor and affective benefits.
3. An improved understanding of the rules of the game.
4. A positive attitude toward the game and an appreciation of its value as a lifetime sport.

COURT DIAGRAM

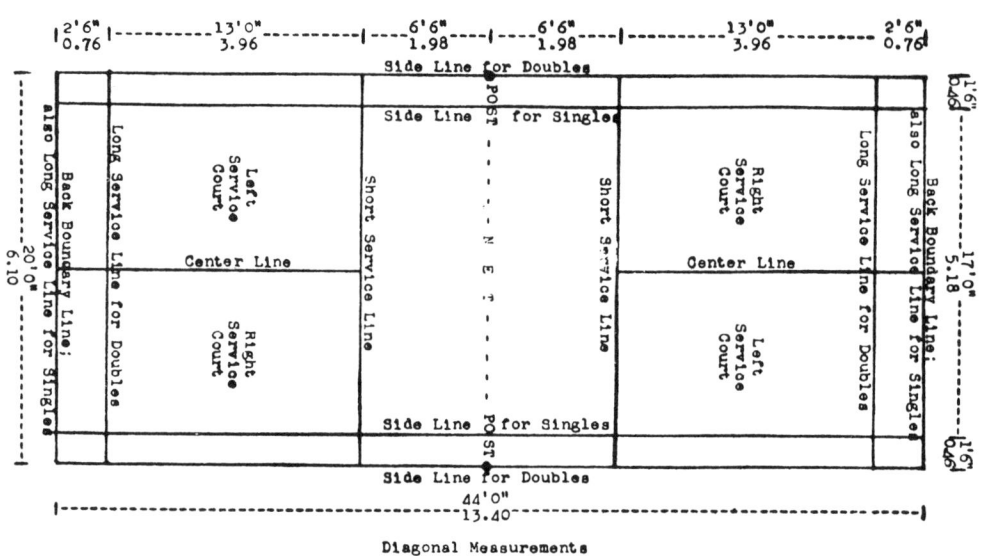

Diagonal Measurements
Full Court (from corner to corner) ... ... 48'4" or 14.723 metres.
Half Court (from post to back boundary line) ... 29'8¾" or 9.061 metres.

SERVICE AREAS

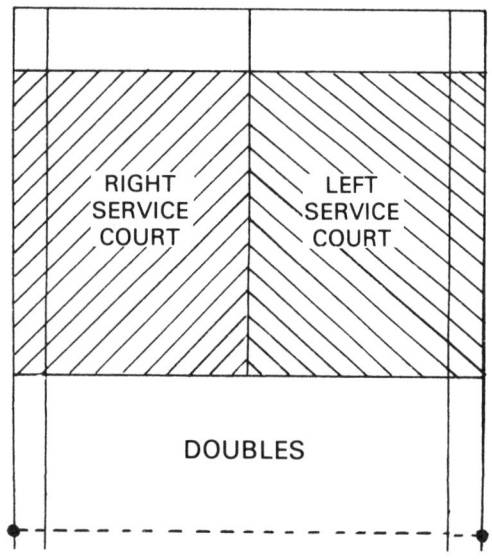

DOUBLES

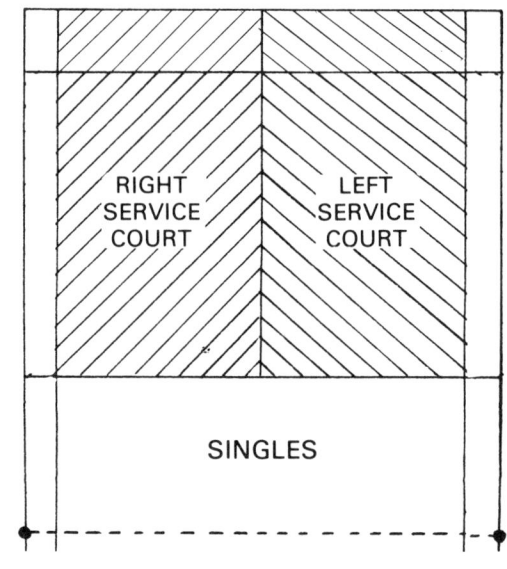

SINGLES

Chapter Two
Skill Development and Teaching Techniques

A. Basic Skills

SKILL	DESCRIPTION	TEACHING TECHNIQUES AND OBSERVATION POINTS

This handbook aims the majority of its information at Level I and Level II skills. Although some Level III and IV material is included, more advanced skill development for small group situations or advanced players may be obtained from the books and audio visual material recommended in the bibliography, or by contacting regional or national coaches listed in the Appendix.

In order to play a game of badminton the players should be able to hit the shuttle both underarm and overhead. On completion of Level I, players should be able to make a low serve, a high serve and an overhead shot using both the proper grip and stroke. All advanced or Level III and IV strokes are refinements of these three basic strokes and the success of all practice drills depends upon their development.

This chapter provides the basic stroke descriptions and common faults associated with the stroke.

1. To avoid distractions during a demonstration have players sit down with racquets and shuttles beside them.
2. Make sure players can see the stroke from all angles.
3. Name the stroke and the area of the court to which it is played.
4. Demonstrate the stroke and explain its uses.
5. Have the players shadow-swing the stroke and correct errors.
6. Introduce footwork. Shadow-swing from waiting position to finished stroke and back to waiting position. Emphasize proper footwork.
7. Stress feeding (hitting bird to proper position) the shuttle properly. Have players hand-feed the shuttle if this is more effective.
8. Use more advanced students as feeders for group drills.
9. Progress from shadow-swinging to stationary hitting to simple moving drills to modified games.
10. Always explain the result and correction of common mistakes so players may help each other.
11. Keep practice sessions interesting by including stationary hitting, drills and modified games so that players at each skill level will gain from the session.

1. Underarm Forehand

The underarm forehand is the basic way to put the shuttle into play.

a) Grip

1. "Shake hands" with the racquet so thumb and forefinger form a "V" on the top edge of the racquet.
2. The thumb and forefinger maintain the proper grip while remaining fingers are in relaxed position on the racquet handle.

SKILL	DESCRIPTION	TEACHING TECHNIQUES AND OBSERVATION POINTS
b) Stroke Components	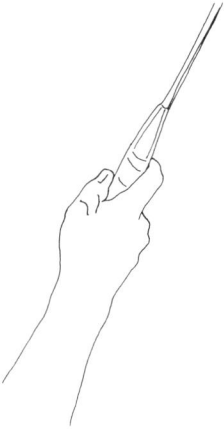	1. The stroke starts from behind the shoulder blades. The body should be turned slightly sideways to the net. 2. The wrist is cocked slightly backward. 3. The racquet is swung at the shuttle so that the arm is straight on contact. 4. The shuttle is contacted in front of the body parallel to the left foot. 5. Follow through with the racquet and body in the direction of the shuttle.
c) Common Faults, Results and Correction		(see table below)

Common Faults	Results	Correction
Wrong grip		
a) Thumb on top of handle	Thumb not gripping racquet Lack of power No control	Check grip regularly Check grip size
b) Forefinger up back of handle	Forefinger not gripping racquet Loss of wrist action and power	
c) Pan-handle (holding the racquet as though it is a frying pan)	Lack of power due to restricted swing	
Inability to contact shuttle	Inability to start rally with an underarm swing	Start with racquet and bird close together in front of body. When player contacts the shuttle, gradually change to the proper stroke
No wrist action	Lack of power	Practice swing without shuttle. Practice bouncing the shuttle on racquet or against a wall
Poor contact point	Misdirected shot Weak return	Move so that the shuttle is contacted at arm's length in front of the body

2. Underarm Backhand

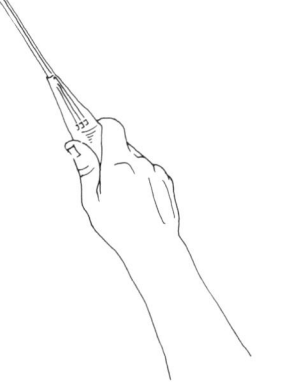

a) Grip

1. The underarm backhand grip varies from the forehand grip in that the thumb is moved from the side of the racquet upwards toward the index finger. This grip adds wrist strength.

b) Stroke Components

1. Waiting in the standard position, the right leg, arm and racquet are brought across the body so that the body is

SKILL	DESCRIPTION	TEACHING TECHNIQUES AND OBSERVATION POINTS
		sideways to the net when contacting the shuttle. 2. The racquet swing starts from behind the shoulders, between waist and chest, with the wrist cocked slightly backward. 3. The point of contact with the shuttle is just in front of the right foot. Racquet arm should be straight. 4. Follow through with the racquet and the body in the direction of the shuttle.
c) Common Faults, Results and Correction		

Common Faults	Results	Correction
Wrong grip	Lack of power	Check grip regularly
No wrist action	Lack of power	Practice swing without shuttle Practice bouncing the shuttle on the racquet or against a wall
Poor body position	Lack of control Lack of power	Make sure the body is turned sideways to the net to allow a proper follow-through

Note: Refined strokes derived from the underarm forehand and backhand include low serve, high serve, drive and net shots.

3. Service

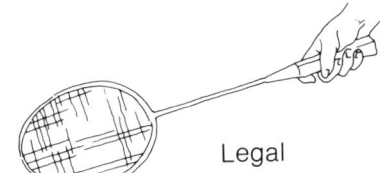
Legal

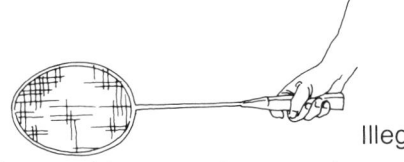
Illegal

a) Governing rules — There are several rules governing any serve in Badminton. They are included here because they affect the development of the service strokes.

1. A service must be an *underarm* swing.
2. When hit, the shuttle must be at, or below, waist level.
3. All parts of the racquet head must be *below* the server's hand at the instant of striking the shuttle.
4. The server is not allowed to walk into the serve or lift his or her back foot off the ground while serving.
5. It is a good shot if the shuttle hits the net on the serve and lands in the proper service court.
6. Once the service stroke is started it must be continuous until the shuttle is hit.

b) Short Serve — The short serve is used mainly in doubles to force opponents to hit shuttle upward.

i Stroke Components

1. Stand a few feet from the front service line with the left foot ahead of the right.
2. Shuttle is held at chest height so it will fall beside the leading foot.
3. Racquet is brought back just behind the racquet hip.

| SKILL | DESCRIPTION | TEACHING TECHNIQUES AND OBSERVATION POINTS |

ii Common Faults, Results and Correction

Elbow is slightly bent. Wrist cocked.
4. Serve is a short, gentle, pushing action.
5. Racquet head is angled upward slightly to direct the shuttle over the net. (See diagram below.)
6. Shuttle is struck at waist height in front of the body.
7. After contact, racquet is swung quickly upward to the waiting position. This enables player to cover loose service returns or pushes.
8. Shuttle should skim the top of the net tape and land just behind the front service line.

Common Faults	Results	Correction
Too much wrist	Shuttle hit too high and/or deep.	Keep wrist cocked. little or no wrist action for short serve
Racquet head angled at ceiling	Upward arm action Trajectory of shuttle not flat enough	Change racquet head angle so serve is more of a sideways push
Starting stroke with racquet forward	Slicing action on shuttle giving loss of control and direction	Start stroke with racquet back
Wrong grip (usually pan-handle with beginner)	Awkward upward arm action Trajectory of shuttle not flat enough	Change grip to basic forehand

c) High Serve

The high serve is an underhand stroke used to put the shuttle into play. It should be high and deep to be useful as a practice feed or Single's serve.

i Stroke Components

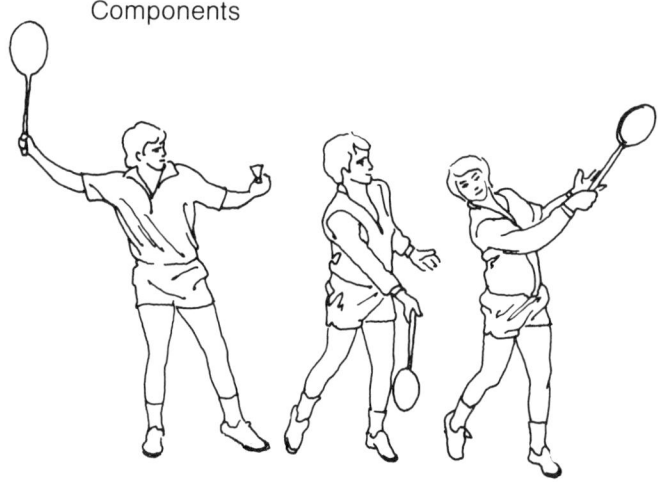

1. Stand relaxed with left foot and left shoulder forward, and right foot behind. Stand a few feet from the short service line.
2. Hold the shuttle at chest height so that it will fall just in front of the non-racquet foot.
3. The stroke is a full underarm swing. Racquet starts well back.
4. The shuttle must be struck when below the waist.
5. The wrist is cocked back at the beginning of the stroke and snaps forward on contact.
6. Follow-through brings the racquet fully across the front of the body and up toward left shoulder. Weight is transferred to left foot.

SKILL	DESCRIPTION	TEACHING TECHNIQUES AND OBSERVATION POINTS

ii Common Faults, Results and Correction

Common Faults	Results	Correction
Snatching at shuttle	Too much wrist follow-through in wrong direction Loss of control Inconsistent serve	Relax Stroke shuttle Use wrist swing to hit shuttle
Standing straight to the net	Awkward position Lack of depth due to poor position for proper follow-through	Start standing slightly sideways to the net and let the body turn as the arm comes forward
Feet too close	Loss of balance causes inconsistent serve	Take up a more comfortable and balanced stance

4. Forehand Overhead Clear

The clear is used to hit the shuttle high and deep from one end of the court to the other. It is mainly a Singles shot to push the opponent to the back court.

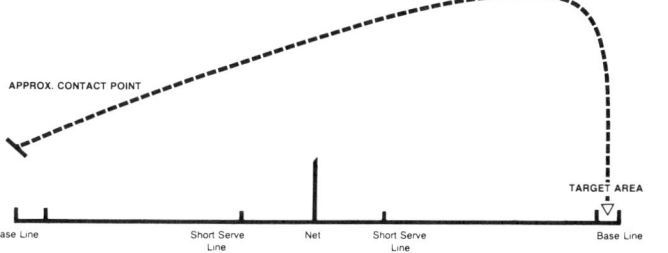

a) Stroke Components

1. Using forehand grip, the racquet is brought back behind the shoulder. Left shoulder points toward the net.
2. Racquet foot is placed behind non-racquet foot and weight is transferred from the back foot to the front foot when hitting the shuttle.
3. Shuttle is hit with a throwing action above the head.
4. The arm is straight at point of impact.
5. Racquet foot moves in front of the non-racquet foot as the stroke is executed so player may move back to center court.

b) Common Faults, Results and Correction

Common Faults	Results	Correction
Shoulders remain square to the net	No transfer of body weight, therefore loss of power	Check grip and footwork. Stand with left shoulder pointing toward net
Shuttle hit with bent arm	Loss of power Flat trajectory	Check height of feed; check grip. Feed high to player and check action.
Shuttle hit to the side of the body	Loss of power Flat trajectory	Check footwork Move body under the shuttle
Feet too close together	Loss of balance No transfer of weight	Practice footwork

SKILL	DESCRIPTION	TEACHING TECHNIQUES AND OBSERVATION POINTS

5. Net Shots

a) Upward Net Shot — Net shots are played very near and just over the net

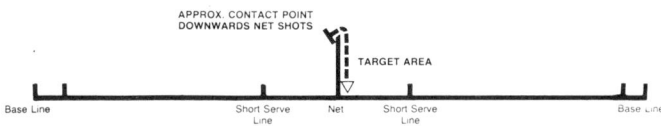

i Stroke Components

1. Racquet arm is slightly bent and the wrist uncocks slightly on impact.
2. Shuttle is met near the top of the net tape, stroked and firmly followed through. The player's racquet should be kept up at tape height after the follow-through.
3. Feet should be one behind the other so the body leans into the shot. Keep head up.

ii Common Faults, Results and Correction

Common Faults	Results	Correction
Shuttle taken too low	Awkward return, upward lift makes defensive shot	Keep racquet head up between shots. Meet shuttle early
Stabbing at shuttle	Loss of control	Stroke the shuttle; lean into the shot in a balanced position
Shuttle carried on racquet	Loss of rally due to fault	Stroke the shuttle

b) Downward Net Shot — This net shot is taken at or above net height. It is a dab, blocking the shuttle so it quickly drops close to, or in front of, the short service line.

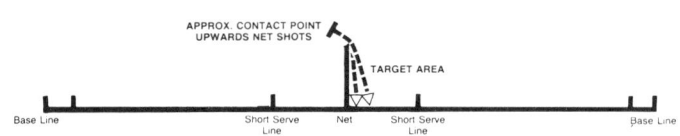

i Stroke Components

1. Use pan-handle grip.
2. Use bent forearm swing, shortened to about .3m in length.
3. Lean into the shot.

ii Common Faults, Results and Correction

Common Faults	Results	Correction
Too little wrist	Shuttle hit out	Use more wrist, hit down, not flat
Late in hitting shuttle	Hit into net	Keep racquet up between shots. Restrict backswing, lean into shot

6. Basic Footwork

a) Ready Position — The waiting position is a mid-court stance.

SKILL	DESCRIPTION	TEACHING TECHNIQUES AND OBSERVATION POINTS
i Position Components		1. Stand with feet approximately shoulder-width apart. 2. Knees are slightly bent. 3. Weight is on balls of the feet. 4. Player returns to this position after hitting each shot. 5. Racquet head is up and in front of the body.
b) Hitting Position	Player should always be behind the shuttle and on balance before the point of contact.	
i Position Components		1. Shuttle should always be hit while the player is on balance. Players should use large steps when running to hit the shuttle. Balance and control are dependent on leg strength and body positioning. 2. For ease of movement, and to ensure a good hitting position, the player should turn slightly sideways to the net when running backward. 3. For overhead shots the hitting position is sideways to the net, with right foot behind left. As the shuttle is hit there is a transfer of weight from back foot to front foot. 4. For net shots, the back foot should be close to the short service line. The front foot lunges to the net to complete the stroke and then pushes off so the player may return to ready position.
ii Common Faults, Results and Correction		(see table below)

Common Faults	Results	Correction
Improper ready position (one foot well in front of other or legs too far apart)	Awkward movement Slow in reaching shuttle Off balance	Check ready position after each stroke
Running straight backwards	Off balance Poor hitting position	Player should turn left shoulder to net each time he or she moves backward
Small steps	Slow movement Awkward hitting position	Practice court movement using wide steps and entire leg
Poor hitting position	Cramped or off balance stroke	Overhead: wait well behind shuttle Net shot: practice lunging for shuttle
Body in front of feet	Awkward Off balance	Increase leg strength Practice taking wide steps Keep body and feet in line

| SKILL | DESCRIPTION | TEACHING TECHNIQUES AND OBSERVATION POINTS |

B. Refined Strokes

1. Overhead Drop Shot

Stroke should be very close to that of an overhead clear. The difference is the position of the racquet head on contact with the shuttle and the amount of wrist used on contact.

Shuttle is directed downward so it falls steeply and lands in the area in front of the short service line close to the net tape.

i Stroke Components

ii Common Faults, Results and Correction

1. Refer to Stroke Components for overhead clear (see p.13).
2. There is a short follow-through along intended line of flight.

Common Faults	Results	Correction
Slow arm action	No deception	Speed up arm action Practice alternating clear and drop
Dabbing at shuttle instead of pulling shuttle down with the racquet	Poor trajectory Slow, defensive shot	Hit shuttle early, reach with a straight arm Get "on top" of shuttle
Striking the shuttle too low	Bent arm action Shoulders square to net Poor trajectory Lack of control	Feed high to player Insist on hitting with a straight arm

2. Smash

The smash is an offensive attacking shot and is used in Singles when the opponent hits a short clear or short drive. It is used in Doubles whenever the shuttle goes up in the air.

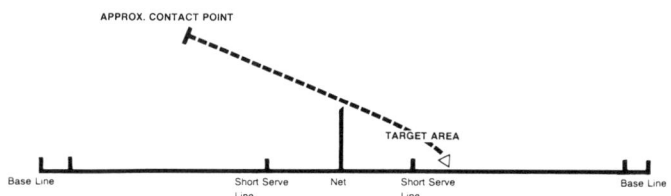

i Stroke Components

1. The smash is the same overhead stroke as the drop shot, only much faster. The angle of the racquet head at impact is the same.
2. The angle and force in the smash are created by greater body rotation and by hitting the shuttle a little sooner.
3. The player must be well behind the shuttle before hitting it to ensure proper use of the body throughout the stroke.

SKILL	DESCRIPTION	TEACHING TECHNIQUES AND OBSERVATION POINTS

ii Common Faults, Results and Correction

Common Faults	Results	Correction
Moving backward while hitting the shuttle	Loss of power Slow recovery Flat trajectory	Check footwork Get well behind shuttle before starting stroke
Hitting shuttle too late	Flat trajectory Loss of power	As above
Bringing shuttle down with the body instead of the racquet	Loss of power Flat trajectory	Reach up; hit shuttle as soon as possible Concentrate on position of racquet head on contact
Dropped elbow	Loss of power Flat trajectory	Think of throwing forearm over elbow

3. Smash Return

The immediate aim of the smash return is to turn the opponent's attacking shot into an offensive shot for the retriever. This is best achieved by moving in from mid-court base to meet the shuttle as early as possible.

i Stroke Components

1. Waiting position for a smash return is with racquet head in front of the body. Wrist is always kept below racquet head.
2. Determine direction of the smash. Only then move to forehand or backhand position.
3. When player knows which side the shuttle is coming to, he or she steps out with that foot and in a balanced position strokes the shuttle back across the net. Racquet head comes across the top of the wrist.
4. Try not to cramp the stroke by contacting the shuttle too close to the body. Get into a good position before hitting the shuttle
5. If the defensive player is fast enough, he or she may change to a pan-handle grip and hit the shuttle with a dab at net height. This type of defense is common in Mixed Doubles.

SKILL	DESCRIPTION	TEACHING TECHNIQUES AND OBSERVATION POINTS		
ii Common Faults, Results and Correction		Common Faults	Results	Correction
		Contacting the shuttle too close to the body	Weak return	Wait with racquet well in front of body. Concentrate on contacting the shuttle well in front
		Committing the racquet to one side	Often caught and unable to hit shuttle	Wait with racquet in ready position
		Hitting the shuttle below waist level	Weak return	Contact at waist level or above, racquet head above wrist

4. Backhand Overhead Clear

(From CBA manual. Used with permission) Backhand is used for shots well on the non-racquet side of the body.

i Stroke Components

1. Player turns body so that back almost completely faces the net. Both feet point toward the back line. Racquet foot is half a stride closer.
2. Racquet head is brought across body. Elbow is bent and pointing at the shuttle. Wrist is cocked so that back of the hand faces the player's face.
3. Elbow swings up toward shuttle and arm is straightened.
4. Shuttle is struck from over right shoulder and wrist snaps on the follow-through. There is little follow-through except the wrist snap since the player must pivot back to the ready position immediately.
5. As shuttle is hit, body weight is transferred from right foot to left foot.

ii Common Faults, Results and Correction

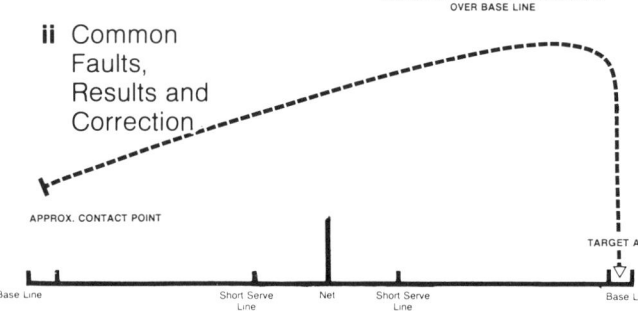

Common Faults	Results	Correction
Wrong grip	Mis-hits and slices	Practice proper grip
Hitting off wrong foot	Poor or no weight transfer	Turn back toward net
Not enough back-swing	Shuttle fails to reach target area	With elbow fully bent, take racquet back across body

5. Stroke Variation

Once a player has learned the basic and refined strokes described above, more variations may be added to the stroke collection by varying the wrist action and the angle of the racquet head on impact. Perfecting these

SKILL	DESCRIPTION	TEACHING TECHNIQUES AND OBSERVATION POINTS
	shots comes at Level III and IV and requires individual instruction.	

i Stroke Components

Stroke Component	Basic Action	Wrist Action Change	Racquet Head Change at Impact	Diagram Number
Flick Serve	Low serve	Wrist snap at last second	Slightly more inclined	One
Drive Serve	High serve	Nil	Flatter angle to net	Two
Underhand Drive	Underhand forehand or backhand	Full wrist snap	Definite angle to net	Three
Underhand Clear	Underhand forehand or backhand	Full wrist snap	Definite angle to ceiling	Four
Overhead Drive	Overhead clear	Nil	Angle flatter, straight at opponent	Five
Backhand Drop (Overhead)	Backhand clear	Slower wrist snap	Angled to floor	Six
Backhand Smash	Backhand clear	Sharp wrist snap	Angled to floor	Seven
Overhead cut shots	Overhead clear	Nil	Sideways cut with racquet	Not shown
Underhand cut shots	Net shots	Nil	Angled slightly to net Chopping action to net	Not shown
Around the head clear	Overhead only over non-racquet shoulder	Nil	Nil	Flight path same as for overhead drive

Note: Cut shots are advanced strokes for Level III, however players should experiment with cuts similar to those used in table tennis or tennis. They will not be discussed in this manual as they are applicable to only a small number of school players.

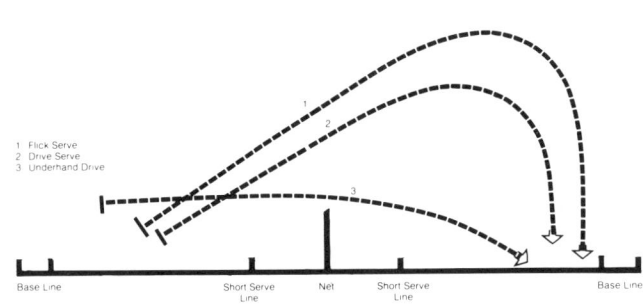

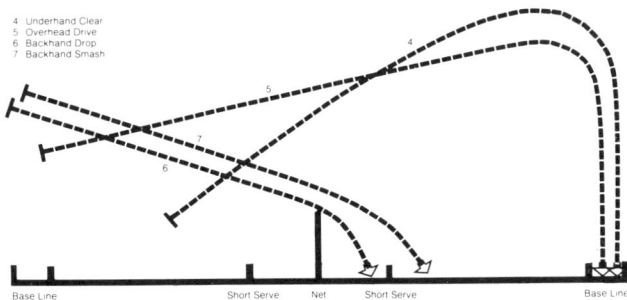

SKILL	DESCRIPTION	TEACHING TECHNIQUES AND OBSERVATION POINTS

C. Rules

The rules described below are in the correct but simple form. For more detailed information instructors should refer to the CBA rules handbook. Refer to page 8 of this manual for court dimensions and service areas.

1. Start of Game

a) Rally, toss and so on --

1. Winner has option of:
   a) Serving first, or
   b) Not serving first, or
   c) Choosing ends.
2. The loser has the choice of any alternative remaining.

b) Serving

1. Each play starts with a service made by an underhand swing with the racquet; that is, the shuttle, when hit, must be at or below waist level.
2. The server stands with both feet in the service court and the shuttle must go over the short service line into the diagonally opposite court without touching the net.

i Singles

1. The players shall serve from their respective right-hand service court only when the server's score is "0" or when server has scored an even number of points in the game.
2. The first serve is from the server's right-hand court to the player in the opposite right-hand court and, if good, the next serve is from server's left-hand court, and so on alternately until a fault is made.

ii Doubles

1. The first service of a side in each inning shall be made from the right-hand service court.
2. To start the game, the player in the right-hand service court of the side which is to have first service, commences the game by serving to the player in the service court diagonally opposite.
3. If the serving side scores a point, the players change from one service court to the other, the service now being from the left-hand service court to the player in the service court diagonally opposite and so on, alternately until the serving side makes a fault.
4. When a fault is made by the serving side, that side is out, since the side beginning the game has only one hand in its first inning (but thereafter has two) so the player in the opposing right-hand service court becomes the server.

SKILL	DESCRIPTION	TEACHING TECHNIQUES AND OBSERVATION POINTS
2. Game		
a) Points played	Best out of three games for a match	
i Singles -	Men - 15 Women - 11	
ii Doubles	Men - 15 or 21 Women - 15 Mixed - 15	
b) Scoring		1. In both Singles and Doubles, the serving side is the only one to score, making its points on the opponent's faults. 2. If the serving side faults, the player is out and the serve passes to the next player.
c) Setting		1. If the score is 13 all, in a game of 15 points, the first side to reach 13 has the choice of "setting" the game to 5 points or playing the remaining 2 points only. 2. If the score is 14 all, the first side to reach 14 has the choice of "setting" to 3 points if, and only if, the score was not set at 13 at all. They may, however, play the remaining one point only. 3. In Ladies' Singles the game is to 11 points. If the score is 9 all, the woman reaching 9 first has the choice of setting the game to 3 points or playing the remaining 2 points. If the score is 10 all, the first woman to reach 10 has the choice of setting 2 points if, and only if, the score was not set at 9 all. She may, however, play the remaining point only.
3. Faults		
a) A player faults:		1. If, in serving, the shuttle at the instant of being struck be higher than the server's waist, or if any part of the head of the racquet, at the instant of striking the shuttle, be higher than any part of the server's hand holding the racquet. 2. If, in serving, the shuttle falls outside the boundary lines of the service court into which service is in order. 3. If, in serving, either the server or receiver stands without both feet in the proper service court. 4. If, before or during delivery of service, any player intentionally distracts his or her opponent. 5. If, either in service or play, the shuttle falls outside the boundaries of court, or passes through or under the net, or fails to pass the net, or touches the roof or side walls, or the person or dress of a player. (A shuttle falling on a line shall be deemed to have fallen into the court or service court of which such line is the boundary.) 6. If the shuttle "in play" be struck before it crosses to the striker's side of the net. (The striker may, however, follow the shuttle over the net with his or her racquet in the course of his or her stroke.)

SKILL	DESCRIPTION	TEACHING TECHNIQUES AND OBSERVATION POINTS
		7. If, when the shuttle is "in play," a player touches the net or its supports with racquet, person or dress.
8. If the shuttle be hit twice in succession by the same player, or be hit by a player and his or her partner successively, or if the shuttle be not distinctly hit or the base of the shuttle be hit by the frame, shaft, or handle of the racquet.
9. If, in play, a player strikes the shuttle (unless he or she thereby makes a good return) or is struck by it, whether he or she is standing within or outside the boundaries of the court.
10. If a player obstructs an opponent.
4. General Rules		1. If, in a service, the shuttle touches the net, it is a "let," provided the service be otherwise good and the serve shall be taken again.
2. If, in a rally, the shuttle touches and passes over the net, it does not invalidate the stroke.
3. If the server in attempting to serve misses the shuttle, it is not a fault; but if the shuttle is touched by the racquet, a service is thereby delivered.

D. Tactics

SKILL	DESCRIPTION	TEACHING TECHNIQUES AND OBSERVATION POINTS
1. Mental Discipline		1. It can be developed through realistic assessment of strengths and weaknesses.
2. Encourage all players, whether beginners or more advanced, to set progressive goals.
3. The goal may be to hit ten consecutive clears to the back line or to win a championship.
a) Self-discipline	An essential tactical tool.	
b) Determination	A key mental quality.	1. Encourage players to keep trying even though progress may be slow.
2. Remind them that during a match the bird dog who is determined to return each shot often wins over more skilled opponents.
c) Concentration	Required for each shot.	1. Remind players that concentration goes hand in hand with consistency and smart game tactics.
2. Players should have a clear idea of what they are doing during a match.
d) Emotional Control	Essential in the game.	1. Becoming upset during a game will affect a player's consistency and tactics.
2. Point out that if an opponent realizes the other player is upset, he or she may use it to tactical advantage. The key is: be calm, cool and collected.
2. Game Tactics	Modified games (Chapter Three) provide an excellent method of teaching tactics since the sequence of shots in those games can	

SKILL	DESCRIPTION	TEACHING TECHNIQUES AND OBSERVATION POINTS
	often be used effectively during a real match. They teach the player to be aware of every shot that is hit.	
a) Defensive and Offensive Play	Whether playing Singles, Doubles or Mixed Doubles, players should know when they are hitting either a defensive or offensive shot.	
i Defensive shot		1. Any shot in an upward direction that gives the opponent a chance to hit it down. 2. A slow shot that gives the opponent ample reaction time; that is, a slow drop, looping clear. 3. A "nothing shot" to mid-court area -- the opponent does not have to move or react quickly. **Note:** *The shots described above can be effective if used occasionally, but remember: Be aggressive. Try to place the shuttle on every hit.*
ii Offensive shot		1. **A smash** -- the hitter must be on balance or a good return by the opponent will make the smash a very defensive shot. 2. **A deep clear** -- although the clear is not traveling in a downward direction, if it is placed deep in the corners it makes the opponent move to one corner of the court and thus sets up a good opportunity for attacking (the chess player's approach.) Most players are least effective when moving backward so the clear may set the opponent off balance. 3. **A fast drop shot** -- this shot changes the speed and/or direction of the shuttle and forces the opponent to move quickly. If the drop does not win the rally, it may cause the opponent to lose balance and/or hit the shuttle upwards. **Note:** *It is important to return to the center after each hit. Assume an offensive stance -- racquet head up; feet slightly apart. Good footwork can be your best offensive tool.*
b) Serve and Serve Return	The most valuable tactical practice an instructor can offer is that of serve and return of serve. Players should practice sequences of serve, serve return and return of return at every practice. It is an easy way for players to see the reason for the outcome of most rallies. The outcome of the entire game is often dependent on these two skills.	

SKILL	DESCRIPTION	TEACHING TECHNIQUES AND OBSERVATION POINTS
i Serve		1. **Singles:** the serve should be high, deep and to the center of the court eighty percent of the time. This forces the opponent to the back of the court and into a position where he or she must hit out toward the sidelines (larger margin for error) in order to make the server move. 2. **Doubles:** the serve should skim the top of the net and land just over the short service line close to the center court line. This forces the receiver to hit the shuttle up (a defensive shot).
ii Return of Serve		1. **Singles;** a deep clear or a fast, steep drop are most effective. 2. **Doubles:** a push shot to the alley or the opponent's body from net height or a tight net shot.
c) Specific Tactics in Singles	Singles play is based to a great extent on excellent physical conditioning; consistent, accurate placement of the shuttle and the ability to maneuver the opponent around the court.	
i Game play		1. The game usually starts with a high, deep serve. It is a duel that forces the opponent out of position and off balance into the corners of the court, causing weak returns that can be smashed to win rallies. 2. Try to develop a good overhead clear to take advantage of length of the court. 3. Make the opponent run as much as possible; that is, diagonally opposite returns, since in most matches where the players are technically equal, physical conditioning can decide the outcome. As physical conditioning deteriorates, so does consistency, accuracy, footwork and the ability to think clearly.

SKILL	DESCRIPTION	TEACHING TECHNIQUES AND OBSERVATION POINTS

ii Common Faults, Results and Correction

Common Faults	Results	Correction
Short high service	Receiver smashes for winner	Improve high service
Short clears	Opponent smashes or drops for winner	Increase length of clears
Too many drops or smashes in return of good high service	Player caught out of position by opponent's return	Clear return of deep high service
Failure to return to center court base	Player cannot cover corners of courts—caught out of position	Return to center court quickly after each shot
Over-use of cross-court shots	Shuttle intercepted to place striker in poor position	Hit cross-court normally when opponent is out of positon on one side of the court
Smashing from base line or when off balance	Inability to cover smash returns	Smash only when well balanced and shuttle in front of doubles service line
Shuttle directed into center of court	Opponent never forced to move out of position	Play shuttle to four corners of the court

★Used with permission of Canadian Badminton Association

d) Specific Tactics in Doubles

i Game Play

1. The key word in doubles is "attack" by hitting the shuttle down. In Ladies' Doubles a deep clear is also an attacking shot. The ability to excel in service and service return is most often the deciding factor in well-contested doubles matches. Use short serves with the occasional flick service to catch the opponent off balance.
2. There are two basic formations in Doubles:
    a) Offensive -- up and back;
    b) Defensive -- side by side.
   Many Doubles teams have trouble switching from offensive to defensive. The initial action when switching to a defensive formation must be taken by the forecourt player because he or she cannot see what his or her partner is doing.
3. Remember that Doubles is a team game. A good Doubles player considers the effect his or her shot has on the partner.

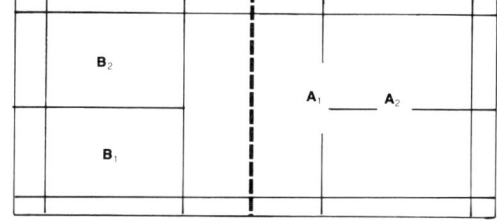

SKILL	DESCRIPTION	TEACHING TECHNIQUES AND OBSERVATION POINTS		
ii Common Faults, Results and Correction		Common Faults	Results	Correction
		High serve used instead of short	Receiver gains immediate attack	Emphasize importance of short serve.
		Server stands too far back	Slow to get to the net for short return	Serve from nearer short service line.
		Receiver hits shuttle upwards	Server and partner gain attack	Move receiver closer to short service line. Use push and drop shots to return short service.
		Shuttle cleared instead of smashed	Attack likely lost (except perhaps in Ladies' Doubles)	Emphasize importance of smash. Adopt attacking formation quickly.
		Clears not deep enough	Opponents kill shuttle	Clear deeply and adopt defence formation.

★Used with permission of Canadian Badminton Association

e) Specific Tactics in Mixed Doubles

i Game Play

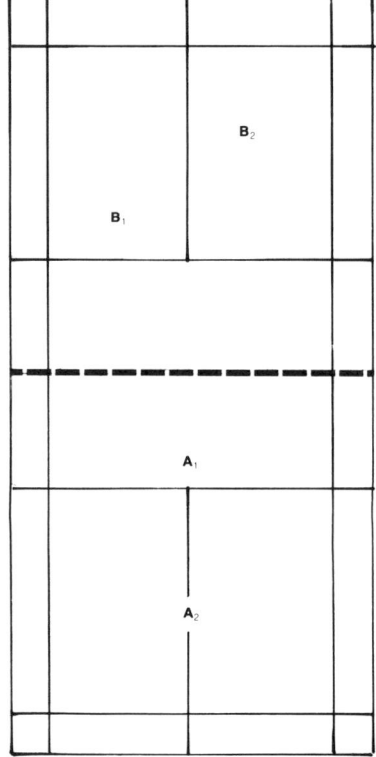

A₁ and B₁ = women

A₂ and B₂ = men

1. In conventional mixed Doubles the woman plays in the forecourt near the Doubles service line; the man plays behind.
2. The woman's strategy is to intercept, and whenever possible she should push the shuttle down just behind the opposing woman.
3. Often the woman's body positioning can take pressure off her partner. For example, in defending a smash the woman should stand about .3m behind the short service line, on the side diagonally opposite from where the attack is being made. In this position she may effectively block most smashes to her court.
4. The man's strategy is to hit the shuttle between the man and woman and to move the man around the back court.
5. As in Doubles, the serve and return of serve are extremely important and can determine the outcome of the match

SKILL	DESCRIPTION	TEACHING TECHNIQUES AND OBSERVATION POINTS		
ii Common Faults, Results and Correction		Common Faults	Results	Correction
		Men driving or clearing to one another continuously	Women out of game. Steadiest or fittest man wins the game	Vary the length of shots. Use push shots past the opposing woman
		Man plays slow drop shots from the back of the court	Waiting woman kills the shuttle	Do not play slow drop shots unless the opponents are out of position
		Clears not deep enough	Woman partner has to duck out of the way as the opponents kill shuttle from half court	Clear deep.
		Woman stands at net with racquet below tape level	Woman slow to intercept	Racquet up
		Man slow to get to push shots	Man hits shuttle up half court; opponents smash shuttle at woman	Intercept shuttle as soon as possible

★ Used with permission of Canadian Badminton Association

Chapter Three
Drills

This chapter provides a selection of drills appropriate to the basic stroke descriptions outlined in Chapter Two. Ideally, an instructor would be able to set aside a court for players who have developed good basic strokes so that they might be able to practice the more complex drills.

Footwork should be emphasized at all times since good footwork will enable players to move quickly into the proper position to hit the shuttle.

With Level 1 players, footwork should be reinforced.

1. Stress footwork drills (See section D). Practice for correct movement without hitting the shuttle.
2. Stop rallies during a game to point out errors and corrections. With more advanced players, skills should be good enough that advanced drills combining stroke practice and footwork practice should complement the above.

A. Practice Drills for Basic Underarm Strokes

Drill	Result	Class Formation
1. Bird Bounce	Practice for proper grip, use of wrist, contact with shuttle	Arrange class in scatter formation. Players practice hitting shuttle up into the air with forehand and backhand. Advanced players may try to hit the ceiling.
2. Wall Hit	Players learn to stroke the shuttle Encourages wrist use	Spread players 2½m (8 ft.) apart facing the wall. Players should be about 1½m (4 ft.) from wall. Players may use lines hitting the shuttle in rotation
3. Hit and Run	Players learn to hit and move quickly	LEVEL I: A single feeder serves high to player "A" who hits the shuttle and goes to the end of the line. The feeder may use several shuttles to keep the rally going. LEVEL II: Two rotating lines. Each player clears the shuttle.

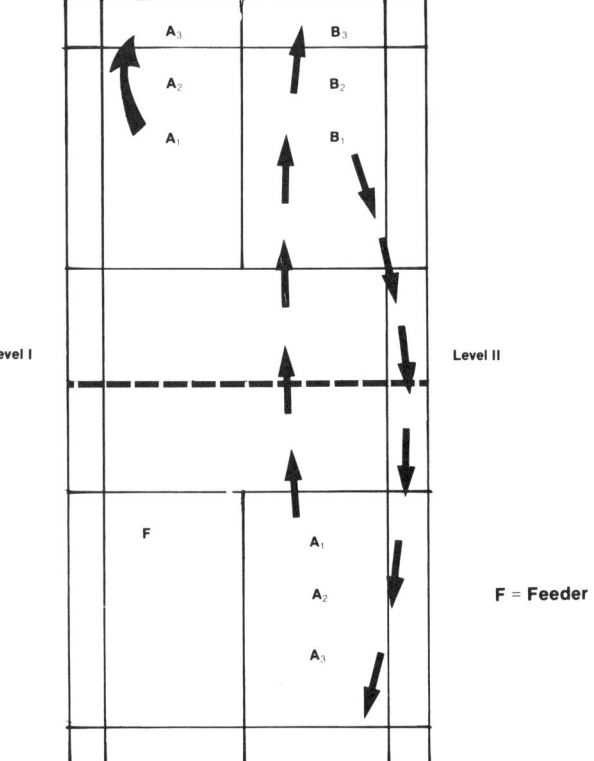

F = Feeder

B. Service Drills

Drill	Result	Class Formation
1. Target Practice	Players learn to hit specific area	One side of each court is marked with service areas. Players take turns serving, and retrieving (see diagram)
2. Between the Ropes	Players learn to keep low serves close to the tape level	A rope or ribbon is fixed across the court .3m above the net height. Players serve so that the shuttle passes between the rope and the net.
3. Serve and Return	Players see immediately how effective their serve is	Working in groups of three: server, receiver and shuttle retriever. Rotate positions every 10 serves

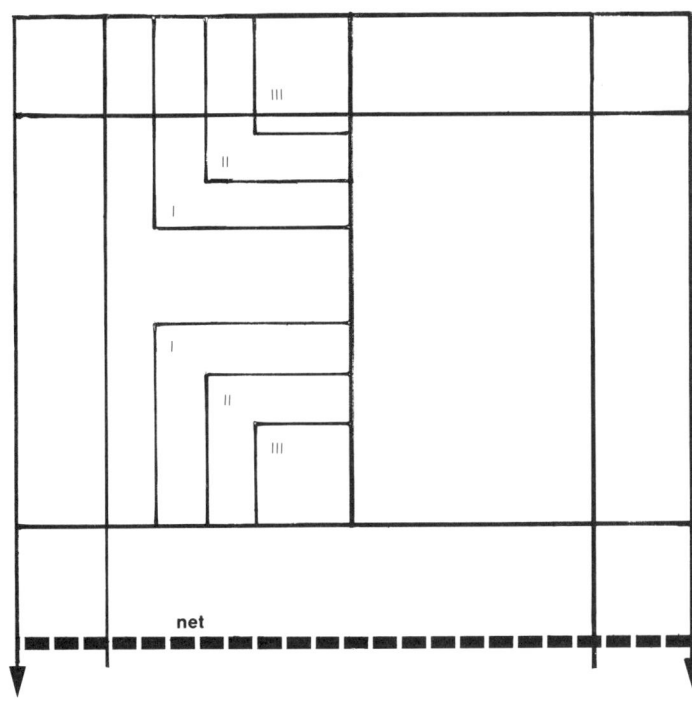

C. Forehand Overhead Clear Drills

Drill	Result	Class Formation
1. "Pig in the Middle"	Players learn to hit the shuttle high	Divide courts into three areas as shown below Players on the outside try to hit shuttle over center person's head
2. Hit and Run	Players learn to react quickly	As described under Hit and Run (p.28)

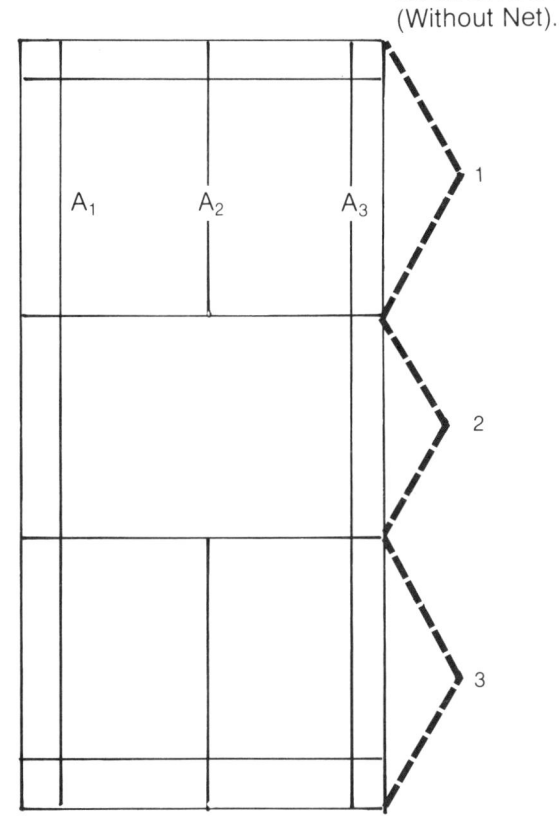

Pig in the Middle

D. Running Drills (Footwork Practice)

Drill	Result	Class Formation
1. Forward and Backward Court Running	Players learn proper footwork while shadow-swinging	Players start at mid-court in ready position. Run forward and lunge for a net shot then run backward and shadow-swing an overhead shot at the baseline (see diagram) Repeat 10 times
2. Side-to-Side Run (without a shuttle or racquet)	Players learn to move sideways using wide steps	Players stand one behind each other straddling center line. They touch right sideline with right hand and then left sideline with left hand. (see diagram) Repeat 10 times
3. Indonesian Reaction	Players learn to react quickly and return to the center after each stroke	Working in pairs, one partner at the net pointing to various areas of the court at random (see diagram). The runner shadow-swings and returns to the center after each hit.
4. Danish Special	Combination of fitness circuit and footwork practice	Players straddle center line. Moving first to the right - step right, left, lunge to touch Doubles sideline with hand. Push off the right leg. Pivot on left leg, step right, left, lunge to touch other Doubles sideline (see diagram) Touch each sideline 10 times. Then do 10 push ups, 10 sit-ups, 10 leg ups. All of the above constitutes one "Danish"
5. English Bird Dog	Improves agility and leg strength Practice for footwork to various court areas	The same as in the Indonesian Reaction, only shuttles are placed at the court positions. Player starts by picking up the shuttle at center court. Moving in a clockwise direction, the player exchanges each shuttle with the center court shuttle. Ideal in relay form

Note: As conditioning improves, repetitions and/or time limitations should be adopted.

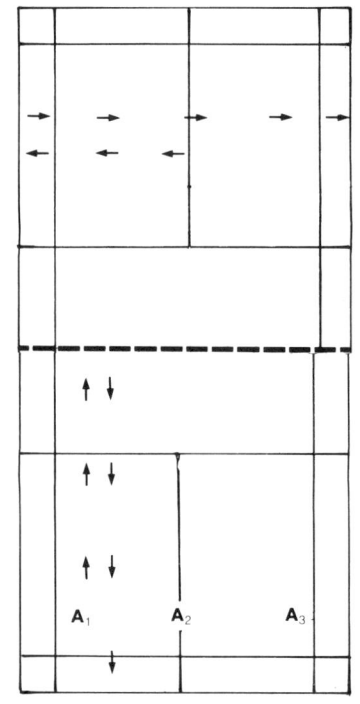

Side to Side Court Running

Forward and Backward Court Running

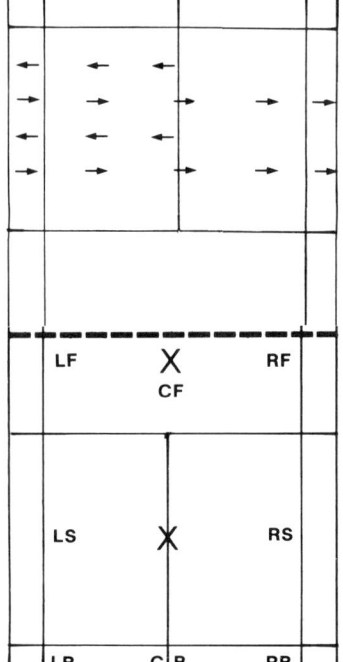

Danish Special

Indonesian Reaction

X = player

E. Net Shot Drills

Drill	Result	Class Formation
1. Net Game	Practice touch	Two players play a game in front of the short service line (four players may practice clears over them).
2. Half-Court Doubles	Practice proper Doubles positioning	Eight players per court. Front player serves the bird. Players switch position when the second player serves. Either player may return serve.
3. Continuous Net	Practice keeping racquet up and moving back to ready position	One player at net. Feeder hits birds in rapid succession to various positions along net

F. Overhead Drop Shot Drills

Drill	Result	Class Formation
1. Stationary Hit	Practice proper action	One feeder-rotating line of hitters, each hits three shuttles then retrieves for the feeder before returning to line-up
2. Alternating Overhead Clear and Drop	Practice keeping similar strokes Feeder may practice footwork	As above. Both drills one and two may be done in pairs if skill and court space are appropriate
3. Modified game Clear, clear, drop	Practice in footwork, deception and thinking	Team Singles on one-half court
4. Two-corner drop	Practice in forward and backward movement while hitting overhead drop shots	Hitter alternates overhead drop and net shots while feeder hits underhand clear, drop drop

G. Smash and Smash Return

Drill	Result	Class Formation
1. Smash Game	Players learn to react quickly	In pairs, on half-court. One player serves high the entire game, then retrieves, preferably with a clear. Other player smashes everything. Rally continues until a fault is made. A point is scored on every rally
2. Two-on-one Attack	Practice for smash and return in Doubles formation	In three s on half-court Single player: defense Doubles players: offense

H. Backhand Overhead Clear Drills

Drill	Result	Class Formation
1. Wall Hit	Continuous fast hitting Increased use of wrist will cause shuttle to bounce off wall	Players spaced evenly around gym about one meter from wall
2. Low-high Feed	Practice getting into proper position from other area of the court	A feeder on one side hits the shuttle to Player A near the net. Player A returns it and moves off court so Player B may have a turn

I. Modified Games

Modified games are an excellent way to bring a practice session closer to a real game situation. Depending on court space, each game may be played on a half or full court. Games may also accommodate more players by using a team concept in which everyone has a partner. One player plays until he or she makes a fault and is then replaced by his or her partner. In this way, as many as eight players may participate in a modified game on a single court. Beginners often have a better game on the half-court since the rallies are longer.

Note: Playing team Singles in modified games allows more players to practice per half-court. In team Singles one player plays the game until a mistake is made at which time he or she is replaced by a partner. This method also rewards players for being able to keep the shuttle in play because, as long as they don't make a mistake, they stay on the court.

Game	Purpose	Rules
Clearing Game	Practice and strengthen overhead clear	Basic rules, but all shots must fall within 2m of the base line
Clear, Clear, Drop	Practice basic strokes, deception, concentration	Basic rules, but rallies must follow the sequence: Clear, Clear, drop.
Drop, Drop, Clear	Reacting to overhead drop and net shots	Basic rules, but rallies must follow the sequence: drop, drop, clear.
Smash Game	Practice in continuous smashing and defense	Basic rules but offensive player attempts to smash everything while server (defensive player) attempts to return with a lift.
Net Game	Practice touch and control at net	Basic rules except all shots must land in front of the short service line.
Timed Games★	Continuous effort, easy organization	Basic rules but a time limit. Leading player wins.
Up and Back Doubles	Practice proper offensive Doubles	Basic rules but one player always front, one player always back. Good on half-court.

Note: Timed games may be applied to any of the other modified games. At the end of the period players rotate in a round-robin fashion or winners may rotate one way, losers the other. If calibre differs among the players, round-robins, each accommodating a skill level may be carried out on separate courts.

Chapter Four
Sample Lesson Plans

These ten lesson plans have been developed as examples of how the skills may be taught. They are designed for Level I - Beginner players and are intended for an activity period of approximately 50 minutes. Each player should have a racquet and there should be one shuttle for every two players.

However, when skill levels vary as they do in most groups, it is important to have something for everyone at every practice. In lessons where a new stroke is introduced, stationary hitting is advised for beginner players, but advanced players can practice the same strokes on the move, returning to ready position at mid-court after each hit.

Advanced players (Levels III and IV) differ from the beginner and novice in that all their actions are much quicker. They get into position more quickly and their strokes are short and efficient. It is very much like handwriting. At first, making letters requires slow, large movements. With practice, writing becomes automatic and the writer uses quick, short, neat strokes. The same refinement process is used in developing badminton strokes. The advanced player can easily take part in stroke practice alongside the beginner. The difference will be in the quality of performance. The advanced player also makes an excellent feeder for less skilled players. Many modified games can include players of varying skills. The advanced player may play against two players instead of one, or may have restrictions such as "no smashing" to make it more of a challenge.

Another way of including several levels in one class is to present the group with a progressive task list at the beginning of each session. Players would spend time practicing each task they are capable of doing. For example:

1. Over-head drop shot
2. Alternating clear and drop, trying to make the strokes similar
3. Two-corner drop drill (see Chapter Three, Drills)

Note to instructor:

1. *Constantly stress grip, quality feeds and footwork.*
2. *Practice some form of serve and return of serve at every session.*
3. *For ease of organization, play timed games rather than a certain number of points.*

Lesson One

1. Introduction
This session will cover the essential background material. Explain the Levels system and the lesson programs; introduce the equipment (racquets, birds, footwear), and initiate some discussion of the social and fitness benefits of the game.

2. Objectives
By the end of the lesson the players should be able to perform the following skills:

a) Demonstrate the proper grip
b) Hit underhand shots
c) Demonstrate hitting and running simultaneously
d) Play a simple game (half-court Doubles)

3. Warm-up - 5 min.
Free hitting to assess abilities

4. Review
For Lesson One this section would be omitted.

5. New Material - 20 min.

a) Have players sit around one court. Demonstrate the proper grip. Check the players' grips.
b) Demonstrate underhand hitting with a forehand and backhand stroke. Using the class positioning illustrated below, have the players practice underhand hitting in pairs.
c) Demonstrate Hit and Run Drill (maximum of six per half-court). Remind players to keep to the outside after hitting the shuttle. Allow players to use underhand or overhead stroke but remind them about using the proper grip.

6. Modified Game

Demonstrate half-court Doubles and explain the rules:

a) Players remain in the front and back positions for the entire rally.
b) The front player always serves the shuttle. Either opponent may return the serve.
c) If the server loses the rally, he or she switches places with partner, who serves the shuttle.
d) If the server wins the rally, a point is scored and he or she serves again.
e) When both players on the serving side have served and lost a rally the serve switches sides.

The game encourages moving the shuttle the length of the court and gives the players an idea of offensive positioning for Doubles.

Lesson Two - Basic Underarm Strokes

1. Introduction

This session will focus on developing the strokes which will be the mainstay of any player's game.

2. Objectives

By the end of this lesson players should be able to:

a) Demonstrate and practice basic underarm strokes: high serve, low serve, net shots.
b) Demonstrate and shadow-swing the proper overhead stroke.
c) Hit the shuttle using the proper overhead stroke.
d) Demonstrate and practice forward and backward court movement.

3. Warm-up - 10 min.

a) Free hitting
b) Forward and Backward Court Running Drill:
  i) Position players mid-court in ready position.
  ii) Players run to back and shadow-swing an overhead, then run to net to shadow-swing a net shot.
  iii) Remind players to move efficiently and to hit when in balanced position.

4. Review - 5 min.

Review through questioning, grip and underarm hits.

5. New Material - 15 min.

a) Demonstrate the low serve, net shot and high serve.
b) Divide the group in half.
  Group A: Practice low serve, net shots and high serve working in pairs. Do not worry about serving diagonally opposite.
  Group B: Teach an overhead throwing motion with and without the racquet. Reverse groups.
c) Organize the group for underhand hitting as illustrated in Lesson One. The feeder hits a high serve. The hitter attempts to return with an overhead. The feeder catches the shuttle and serves again.

6. Modified Game - 20 min.

Half-court Doubles Round-Robin. Set up a round-robin on each court to split up the skill levels. Play timed games.

Lesson Three - Underhand and Overhead Basic Stroke

1. Introduction

This session continues to introduce the all-important basic strokes.

2. Objective

By the end of this lesson, players should be able to:

a) Demonstrate front, back and side-to-side court movement.
b) Demonstrate underhand and overhead basic strokes.
c) Demonstrate a high serve.
d) Play a simple half-court team Singles game. Make a high serve compulsory.

3. Warm-up - 10 min.

Use a drill designed to practice underarm strokes — Bird Bounce, Wall Hit or Hit and Run (see Chapter Three).

4. Review - 10 min.

a) Review front and back court movement.
b) Review the proper overhead stroke.

5. New Material - 10 min.

a) Introduce side-to-side movement using the Side-to-Side Run Drill.
b) Demonstrate a good feed and a good clear in an overhead stroke.
c) Organize group with eight per court (if necessary), so that four players practice net shots and four players hit practice clears over the net players. Reverse. If players lack control with the overhead, revert to the two-hit rally (serve, hit, catch).

6. Modified Game

Half-court Doubles Round-Robin. Set up a round-robin on each court to split up the skill levels. Play timed games.

Lesson Four - Game Rules

1. Introduction

This session will introduce the rules and etiquette of the game so that players can begin to play their strokes with more understanding and purpose.

2. **Objectives**

By the end of this lesson, the player should be able to:

a) Demonstrate refined ways of hitting the shuttle.
b) Demonstrate basic skills and experiment with advanced skills.
c) Explain the rules of the game scoring and court etiquette.
d) Play a full-court Doubles game.

3. **Warm-up - 10 min.**

Indonesian Reaction Drill (see Chapter Three). Let each player try the drill twice for 30 seconds.

4. **Review - 5 min.**

Review, through questioning and then through player demonstration, varied court movement.

5. **New Material - 20 min.**

a) Demonstrate overhead drop shot, smash, overhead backhand and drive. Emphasize the similarity of the strokes and the differences in the angle of the racquet face on contact.
b) Divide the group in half.

Group A: Working in pairs, experiment with the refined strokes.
Group B: Study a rule sheet.

Reverse groups.

c) Explain proper Doubles scoring through a demonstration Doubles game.

6. **Modified Game - 15 min.**

Timed, full-court Doubles game.

Lesson Five - Skills Test Practice

1. **Introduction**

This session is intended to prepare players for a skills test (see Chapter Five for an explanation of the test, the purpose and the four stations).

2. **Objectives**

By the end of this lesson, players should be able to:

a) Answer questions on the rules and etiquette.
b) Demonstrate all basic skills.

3. **Warm-up - 10 min.**

Hit and Run Drill using specific shots.
Indonesian Reaction Drill--each player has two, 45-second turns.

4. **Review - 5 min.**

Question players on rules. Review court etiquette. Announce rules test for next class.

5. **New Material - 10 min.**

a) Explain Level I skills test.
b) Announce skills test for next class.

6. **Modified Game - 25 min.**

Divide into four groups for practice of test skills. Rotate the groups allowing five minutes at each station.

Lesson Six - Evaluation of Court Skills

1. **Introduction**

In this session, player progress in motor and cognitive areas will be assessed.

2. **Objectives**

By the end of this lesson, players will be able to demonstrate their command of game rules and court skills.

3. **Warm-up and Review- 10 min.**

Set up the four stations (see Chapter Five) and allow players to practice skills for Level I test.

4. **New Material - 40 min.**

Divide the class into two. One group writes a rules test while the other group does the skills test. Reverse. Allow 20 minutes for each station.

Lesson Seven - Overhead Drop and Smash

1. **Introduction**

This session introduces some advanced shots and the first elements of strategy so that players begin to play a more sophisticated game.

2. **Objective**

By the end of this lesson players should be able to:

a) Demonstrate the overhead drop and smash.
b) Demonstrate serve and return serve.
c) Demonstrate some understanding of Doubles strategy.
d) Demonstrate defensive and offensive positioning.

3. **Warm-up - 5 min.**

Divide players into two groups and organize relays—skipping and/or forward-backward running.

4. **Review - 5 min.**

Review overhead drop shot and smash through questioning and demonstration.

5. **New Material - 10 min.**

a) Divide the class into two groups.

Group A: Practices drop and smash. Use the advanced players as feeders. Work with one feeder and two or three hitter per half-court.

Group B: On one court explain Doubles strategy. Emphasize the importance of serve and return of serve. Demonstrate offensive and defensive positioning.

b) Practice Serve and Return Drill (six players per full court for proper diagonal serves or four players per half-court for straight serves). One player serves ten consecutive serves. The other players in the group return two serves each then collect shuttles for the server. Each player has a turn at being the server.

6. Modified Game - 20 min.

Timed, full-court Doubles.

Students not playing choose someone who is playing and count how many service or service return errors their player makes.

Lesson Eight - Strategy (Multi-Level Lesson)

1. Introduction

In this session, the rules test (from Lesson Six) will be returned, common errors reviewed, and more advanced strategy planning introduced. This lesson is designed for a multi-level class.

2. Objective

By the end of this lesson, players should be able to:

a) Demonstrate proper Doubles positioning and strategy.
b) Play a full-court round-robin.

3. Warm-up - 10 min.

Free hitting. Other footwork drills described in Chapter Three.

4. Review - 5 min

Return rules test and review common errors.

5. New Material - 20 min.

Demonstrate Two-on-One Attack Drill on half-court. The single player feeds high and then defends. The Doubles team stays in front and back positioning and tries to hit the shuttle down. For best results have one strong player defend the court against two weaker players. Weaker players may switch positions every five rallies.

6. Modified Game - 15 min.

Up and Down Doubles. This game is a good way of determining various levels as top players will end up at one end of the gymnasium. Players play timed games. At the end of the time period all winners move in one direction, losers the other. The top team remains in a constant position.

Lesson Nine - Review (Multi-Level Lesson)

1. Introduction

This session provides a multi-level lesson. It is designed as a review of Doubles positioning.

2. Objective

By the end of this lesson, players should be able to:

a) Demonstrate quick reaction at the net, through continuous net play.
b) Demonstrate improved serve and return of serve.
c) Play full-court Doubles.

3. Warm-up - 5 min.

a) Free hitting
b) Danish Special Drill. All players should do two sets. Advanced players should do an extra set of Side-to-Side Run Drills in the same time period.

4. Review - 5 min.

Review Doubles positioning, emphasizing the duties of the net player.

5. New Material - 20 min.

a) Demonstrate the continuous net drill. Players are in groups of five per court. One player (the hitter) waits in ready position on the shot service line. Two players (the feeders) hit shuttle continuously at the hitter from the opposite side of the net (like a ball machine in tennis). Two or more players retrieve shuttles from the floor and return them to the feeders. Each player has a one-minute turn at the net.
b. Set up markers on the court, as targets for Doubles service returns. Players take turns serving and returning serve, using self-evaluation as part of the drill.

6. Modified Game - 20 min.

From previous game and test results, divide the class into equal groups and play timed game round-robins.

Note: Following these nine lessons, the instructor should evaluate the skill level of the players and adapt future lessons accordingly.

Chapter Five
Evaluation

Continuous personal evaluation is a sign of self-discipline and dedication and will be most effective as long as both the immediate and long-term goals are realistic. An instructor may use either subjective or objective evaluation to determine the level of an individual player or the entire group.

A. Program Evaluation

The success of the program can be judged by the players' response, their progress rate and how much they enjoy playing the game. Their enjoyment may be determined by the extent of participation outside of Physical Education class time. The number of players who turn out for club or team games, or for social round-robins organized outside school hours, would be a good indication of success.

B. Player Evaluation

Player evaluation should incorporate the psychomotor, cognitive and affective objectives as outlined in Chapter One.

1. Psychomotor Evaluation:

This form of evaluation may be conducted by using specific skill testing and/or through game results

- Evaluate each skill by setting up target areas on the court and have players attempt to hit the target area, using specific strokes.
- Use the results of modified games.

a) Objective

Psychomotor Test - Level I - This test is an adaptation of the National Test Program developed by the Canadian Badminton Association.
1. An entire class may be tested at once.
2. Requirements: Three courts
        Instructor or Level II player
        Three player assistants
3. Test includes four stations; three with courts, one that is set up on the back third of the two serving courts.

Station One

Short serve: One mark per serve.
1. Place a marker .5m from the service line.
2. Each player serves five shuttles.
3. Shuttle must land in proper service court within .5m of short service line and not more than .5m above net.

Station Two

High Serve: One mark per serve.
1. Each player serves five shuttles.
2. Shuttles must land within .5m of Doubles service line at back of the court.
3. Shuttles must reach height of 2m at some point during the serve.

Station Three

Overhead stroke: One mark per stroke.
1. Level II player feeds ten high clears to player.
2. Player must return shuttle at least half-court using proper overhead stroke.

Station Four

Forward and backward running: each player starts with five marks.
1. Use area behind serving stations.
2. Player runs forward, shadow-swings net shot; runs backward, shadow-swings overhead shot.
3. Each player does this run three times.
4. Marks deducted for: improper hitting position, loss of balance, awkward footwork.

Total Objective: 25 marks

   b) Subjective

An alternative method of psychomotor evaluation would be to evaluate a player's strokes using subjective psychomotor evaluation. The following checklist may be used as an example:

Each item is evaluated on a scale of 1 to 5 (5 meaning well-executed) with a written comment on weaknesses in each area.

Use of Court Space

___ 1. The space of the court is covered well.
___ 2. The shuttlecock is contacted while in front of the body.
___ 3. An overhead swing is used whenever possible.
___ 4. The shuttlecock is directed to an open space when advantageous
___ 5. The player quickly resumes the ready position after contacting the shuttlecock.

Use of Proper Strokes

___ 1. Wrist action is used to produce the desired stroke.
___ 2. A variety of strokes is used.
___ 3. Serves are effective and accurate.
___ 4. The shuttlecock is contacted as soon as possible.

___ 5. The player considers the opponent's weaknesses in his or her strategy.

Player's greatest strength:

Player's greatest weakness:

2. Cognitive Evaluation:

Specific questions may indicate how knowledgeable the player is about the game of Badminton. The questions could take the form of an oral or written quiz:

   a) Include the sample written test below (15 marks).

      Answer true or false to the following questions. Any questions that are false you are to correct in the space provided.

   1. The service area in Doubles is long and wide.
   2. In badminton, the final score could be 18-16.
   3. In badminton, you have to win by 2 points.
   4. In Doubles, the player who starts in the right court will serve from the right court, when he/she is serving and the score is 10-10.
   5. In Doubles, the receivers change courts when their opponents score a point.
   6. In Doubles, the player who starts in the left court will serve from the right court, when he/she is serving and the score is 8-3.
   7. In Doubles, Player A is serving. The server's partner must stand in his/her own court when Player A is serving. (that is, Player A stands in the right court and Player B stands in the left court.)
   8. In Singles, the court is long and narrow.
   9. In Singles, the service court is short and narrow.
  10. If the bird hits the net on the serve, the server must re-serve the shuttle.
  11. In Singles, when a player gains the serve, he/she always serves first from the right court.
  12. Draw a badminton court. Shade in the Doubles service court on one side of the net and label it. Shade in the Singles service court on the other side of the net and label it.

   b) *Rules Test for Level I*

     i Test for basic rules.
     ii Test court boundaries

     15 marks

Note: It is unlikely that an entire class would reach Level II so group testing as described for Level I may not be appropriate. Play developing Level II skills may be tested using the National Test program.

3. Affective Evaluation

For this sample test, 20% is allowed for subjective evaluation by the instructor. The player is evaluated in the areas of attitude, active participation in the teaching unit, cooperation, sportsmanship and leadership.

Appendix I
Reference Material

A. Books

Canadian Badminton Association. *Local Coaches Manual* and *Regional Coaches Manual Level II*, Canadian Badminton Association, 1976.

Davis, Pat. *The Badminton Coach,* Kaye & Ward Limited, London, 1970.

Friedrich, John and Rutledge, A. *Beginning Badminton,* Wadsworth Publishing Co., Inc., Belmont, California, 1966.

Gregory, D.R. and Webb, G.A. *Teaching Badminton,* Surrey, England, 1972.

Rogers, Wynn. *Advanced Badminton,* Wm. C. Brown Co., Iowa, 1970.

Additional reading lists and films may be obtained from the Canadian Badminton Association, 333 River Road, Ottawa, Ontario, Canada K1L 8B9.

B. Audio Visual Resources

Badminton Series (Video)
  Grip, Footwork, Serves

  Basic Strokes

  Basic Strategy and Drills

These are available from:

  Provincial Education Media Centre
  7451 Elmbridge Way,
  Richmond, B.C. V6X 1B8

C. Badminton Associations

Canada

Canadian Badminton Assoc.
333 River Road
Ottawa, Ont
K1L 8B9

B.C. Badminton Assoc.
Box 3297
Vancouver, B.C.

Alberta Badminton Assoc.
c/o Mrs. P. Ingall
8004 144th Street
Edmonton Alberta
T5R 0R4

Saskatchewan Badminton Assoc.
c/o Keith Biesenthal
Box 625, Grenfell, Sask.
S0G 2B6

Manitoba Badminton Assoc
c/o Jack McDonald
319 Montrose Street
Winnipeg, Manitoba R3M 3M1

Ontario Badminton Assoc.
559 Jarvis Street
Toronto, Ontario M4Y 2J1

Quebec Badminton Assoc.
Gilles Lepage
8566 Rue Rejane
Lasalle, Quebec H8N 1Z1

New Brunswick Badminton Assoc.
Lorne Wortman
Box 1272
Moncton, N.B.

Nova Scotia Badminton Assoc.
E.W. Scratton
57 Melwood Ave.
Halifax, N.S.

Prince Edward Island Badminton Assoc.
Earle Smith
29 Goodwill Ave.
Charlottetown, P.E.I.

Newfoundland Badminton Assoc.
John Hall
6 Gambier St.
St. John's, Newfoundland

Yukon Badminton Assoc.
27 Klondike Rd.
White Hace
Y1A 3L8

N.W.T. Badminton Assoc.
Mrs. P. Curtis
Box 1651
Inuvik, N.W.T.

U.S.A.

Oregon Badminton Assoc.
c/o Mrs. L. Cicirich
1415 Northeast Jarrett
Portland, Oregon

California Badminton Assoc.
c/o Mr. West Shoppe
657 25th St.
Manhatten Beach, California 90266

American Badminton Association
Phone: 313-655-4502

Appendix II
National Test Program

The NTP is a developmental program of the CBA. Its objectives are:

1. To acquaint large numbers of young players with the game of badminton, and to interest them in it.
2. To develop players to a pre-competitive level with the basic understanding and ability to hit most of the fundamental shots of badminton.
3. To provide a framework and guide for certified coaches, school teachers and others who want to coach badminton.

It is a well-organized program, including written tests and instructions for skills testing. Unfortunately, it is dependent on testing one student at a time.

The material covered by each test is as follows:

1st Test

a) Singles serve
b) Overhead forehand
c) Backhand drive
d) Demonstrate correct forehand grip.

2nd Test

a) Demonstrate the "Ready Position"
b) Low Doubles serve
c) Backhand drop shot down-the-line
d) Forehand drop shot down-the-line
e) Footwork exercise--moving to four corners of court.

3rd Test

a) Forehand clears
b) Smash
c) Smash return.

4th Test

a) Alternate down-the-line and cross-court forehand shots followed by a net shot return.
b) Alternate down-the line and cross-court backhands followed by a net shot return.

5th Test

a) Rush a low Doubles serve
b) Smash high Doubles serve
c) Hit flat forehand drives both down-the-line and across court
d) Hit flat backhand drives both down-the-line and across court.
e) Play a game of Singles showing good form and footwork and knowledge of rules.

   Note: Backhand clears and smashes were omitted because they are too advanced for beginner's level. Around-the-head shots are not included for they are merely adaptations of the forehand in Test 1 and 3.

   Note: Additional information and testing kits may be obtained through:

   Canadian Badminton Association
   333 River Road
   Ottawa, Canada   K1L 8B9